Oldham County Public Library System

Overdue notices are a courtesy
of the Library System.

Failure to receive an overdue notice
does not absolve the borrower of
the obligation to return the materials
on time.

THE NEW CREEPY CRAWLY COLLECTION

BEES

For a free color catalog describing Gareth Stevens' list of high-quality books and multimedia programs, call 1-800-542-2595 (USA) or 1-800-461-9120 (Canada). Gareth Stevens Publishing's Fax: (414) 225-0377.
See our catalog, too, on the World Wide Web: http://gsinc.com

Library of Congress Cataloging-in-Publication Data

Fisher, Enid.
   Bees / by Enid Fisher ; illustrated by Tony Gibbons.
      p.   cm. -- (The New creepy crawly collection)
   Includes bibliographical references (p. 24) and index.
   Summary: Describes the physical characteristics, nests, social behavior, role in pollination, and other aspects of bees.
   ISBN 0-8368-1576-9 (lib. bdg.)
   1. Bees--Juvenile literature. [1. Bees.] I. Gibbons, Tony, ill. II. Title. III. Series.
QL565.2.F56 1996
595.79'9--dc20   95-54107

This North American edition first published in 1996 by
Gareth Stevens Publishing
1555 North RiverCenter Drive, Suite 201
Milwaukee, Wisconsin 53212 USA

This U.S. edition © 1996 by Gareth Stevens, Inc. Created with original © 1995 by Quartz Editorial Services, 112 Station Road, Edgware HA8 7AQ U.K.

Consultant: Matthew Robertson, Senior Keeper, Bristol Zoo, Bristol, England.

Printed in Mexico

1 2 3 4 5 6 7 8 9 99 98 97 96

THE NEW
CREEPY CRAWLY
COLLECTION

BEES

by Enid Fisher

Illustrated by Tony Gibbons

Gareth Stevens Publishing
MILWAUKEE

Contents

Getting to know bees

Buzz, buzz, buzz-zz, bu-bu-buzz. Zz. Zz. If you hear that sound on a warm summer's day, chances are it's a bee hovering over a flower after a giant drink of nectar! You'll know it, too, by its furry, striped body. The bee is probably collecting nectar to make honey.

There are over twenty thousand different types of bees. The ones we usually see are bumblebees and honeybees. They are certainly fascinating creatures, and there are lots of questions to ask about them.

For instance, are all bees "busy?" How harmful is their sting? How do they make honey? And why is the queen bee so important?

You can find out all about the life of a bee on the pages that follow.

A busy body

Bees may appear to have soft bodies. But underneath their furry outer covering is a hard shell. This shell covers the bee's entire body, which has three parts.

First, let's take a look at a bee's head. The tongue is called a *proboscis*, and the bee uses its proboscis to reach deep inside flowers and suck out nectar. The bee has three small eyes at the front of its head, and two large eyes, one on each side, as in the illustration here. Amazingly, the two large eyes have over 6,000 lenses each, so the bee can see all around, not just in front. This is very useful, since a bee often has to spot food from a great distance and also check that there is no enemy nearby waiting to pounce and gobble it up.

The inside of a bee's nest is dark, so the bee finds its way by using two antennae at the front of its head. It can pass messages to another bee by tangling its antennae with the other bee's.

The second part of the bee's body is the thorax, or chest cavity, which supports six legs. The back legs have wide, flat parts, fringed with long hairs. These are called *baskets*, and they are specially designed for carrying pollen.

Bees have a double set of wings. There are two main wings (forewings) and two smaller ones (hind wings). The bee makes the familiar buzzing sound that tells you it is near by moving its wings.

The third part of a bee's body is the abdomen. In female bees, this contains the bee's wax-making glands and its only means of protection — the stinger! Poison is kept at the ready in a long tube just under the end of its tail.

So beware, and try to stay very still if a bee buzzes around you! If you ignore the bee, chances are it will ignore you, too, and go away.

Female

Worker bees are very important to the life of the hive. Without them, there would be no hive and no honey to enjoy. But although they are all females, the workers cannot lay eggs — only the queen bee lays eggs.

While very young, worker bees are kept endlessly busy. They help clean out the nest and keep it that way. They collect nectar from older bees and feed it to the hungry bee babies, as shown in the illustration on the right. Once they have grown a little, the young bees are sent to guard the nest entrance.

There may be as many as sixty thousand workers in just one colony! These workers eventually become *foragers* that find flowers and collect nectar and pollen from them. When they have as much as they can carry, the foragers return home to unload it all, repeating the task throughout the day until it gets dark.

workers

After dark, these hard-working females can finally rest. But they will have to be up with the sun, ready to go out and search for the next day's food.

A nest or hive of bees needs hundreds of females to keep it going.

The workers plot their course away from and back to the nest by the angle of the sun. They can also let each other know about the location of nectar by doing a special dance. If they do a round dance, the nectar is nearby. If they dance in the shape of a figure eight, however, this means the nectar is far away.

Male honeybees, which are larger and fewer in number, are known as *drones*. The drones do not work at all. Their only task is to mate with the queen bee so she can lay eggs from which the next generation of bees will hatch. Once this has been accomplished, the female honeybees push the drones out of the nest to starve.

But even worker bees have a short life. Honeybee workers, for instance, live only an average of about six or seven weeks. Worker bees never seem to waste a minute, though! No wonder we have the phrase "as busy as a bee!"

Let's meet

"**I**'m the honeybee queen, and I'm in charge of the hive. You can see me in the center of this picture. Without me, there wouldn't be any other bees. I am the only bee that can lay eggs, so the others care for me all day, cleaning and grooming me, and making sure I have plenty to eat.

"**I**'m nearly twice the size of other bees. As a baby, I was fed mountains of rich food called royal jelly, which my workers produce in their bodies.

"**A** queen bee like me can live for four or five years, much longer than other bees. I rarely leave the hive, except for mating, and I fly out only to attract a drone with my scent. We mate in flight, and then I return to the hive.

"**L**aying thousands of eggs takes up most of my time. I lay each egg in a safe place of its own. My worker bees build thousands of six-sided chambers.

10

the queen

"These chambers, or *cells*, are made of wax. They form what bee experts call the *comb*. I back up into each cell and lay one tiny egg, about the size of a pinhead, in each.

"After three days, the eggs hatch into grubs, or larvae. Worker bees feed them on royal jelly to help them grow. But they only get a little jelly so the female bees will not develop into queens. Only one queen rules the hive, and that's me!

"In only nine days, the larvae have grown so big that they fill the cells. They gradually change into pupae, looking more and more like bees every day. Twelve days pass before they are mature enough to chew their way out of their waxy cells.

"Soon, my hive will be full to bursting with bees. When there's hardly room to breathe, it's time to go. My workers gather around me, and we all leave together to start a new colony."

11

Inside

If you come across a scruffy-looking blob of mud and grass about the size of a soccer ball, then you may have found a bee nest!

Don't be tempted to touch it, though, because bees can give nasty stings if they are disturbed.

The bee nest may not look particularly interesting from the outside, but a lot is going on inside. The queen lies at the center of the nest. Other bees guide her toward the empty cells. She lays a tiny egg in each cell.

Elsewhere in the nest, workers are breathing on the nectar they have gathered with their proboscis. They do this to evaporate water in the nectar as part of the honeymaking process. Then they put it in special cells a little farther back in the nest.

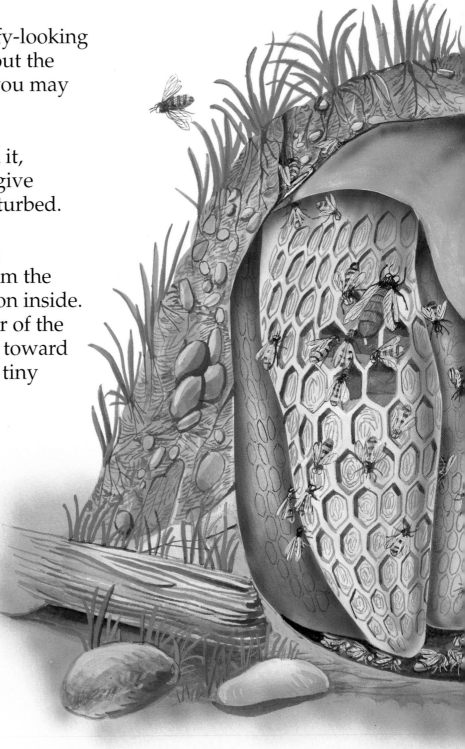

a nest

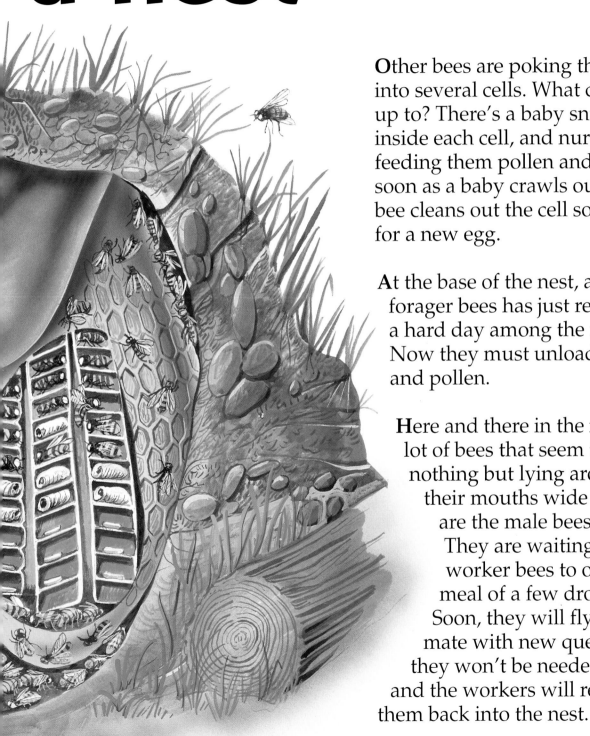

Other bees are poking their heads into several cells. What can they be up to? There's a baby snuggled up inside each cell, and nurse bees are feeding them pollen and nectar. As soon as a baby crawls out, a nurse bee cleans out the cell so it is ready for a new egg.

At the base of the nest, a cluster of forager bees has just returned from a hard day among the flowers. Now they must unload the nectar and pollen.

Here and there in the nest are a lot of bees that seem to be doing nothing but lying around with their mouths wide open. These are the male bees, or drones. They are waiting for passing worker bees to offer them a meal of a few drops of nectar. Soon, they will fly away to mate with new queens. Then, they won't be needed anymore, and the workers will refuse to let them back into the nest.

Delicious

Just about everyone loves honey or jam on bread. Jam, of course, is humanmade from fruits, such as strawberries. But honey is made by the honeybee, whose scientific name is *Apis*.

Hives are usually placed where there are plenty of flowers and trees. At first, a few forager bees leave the hive in search of the sweet nectar and pollen dust in the flowers.

From the word *Apis* comes *apiary*, the name given to a place where bees are kept by a beekeeper, most often a collection of hives. Someone who keeps bees for making honey is known as an *apiarist*.

When they have found a place with plenty of food, these bees return to the hive to tell the others. The information is communicated by means of a dance that contains secret clues.

treats

The forager bees may move around quickly in small circles. This means the flowers are less than 80 feet (25 m) from the hive.

Each bee stores nectar in a special stomach, called a *crop* or *honey-stomach*, in its body. Once this is full, the bee goes back to the hive.

If they perform a dance in the shape of a figure eight, then the bees have to look farther away, perhaps as far as 330 feet (100 m).

Honeybees can crawl right inside the flower to lick the nectar with their long proboscis.

The bees in the hive then work on the nectar. They breathe on it to evaporate the water in it. When the runny nectar becomes thick and sticky, the bees carry it into special chambers, or cells. After a few days, the beekeeper, or apiarist, can lift out the honey-combs and remove the honey. It's then ready for spreading and eating. Delicious!

Beekeeping

What fun it would be to keep a small hive! You have to follow certain rules, though, since the bees can sting. A local beekeeper's association would probably give advice and help, if your family agrees to the idea.

A basic hive is usually a wooden box divided into one brood chamber, where the queen lays her eggs, and at least three honey chambers. Here, flat wooden frames are placed about 1 1/5 inches (3 centimeters) apart to allow the bees to move freely between them.

The bees come and go through a narrow gap at the top or bottom of the hive. A small platform in front of the opening makes takeoff and landing easier for the bees.

So how can you get started? Some beekeepers get permission to go out looking for a swarm of hundreds of bees, usually in a tree, and gently trap the bees in a suitable box.

Then they move the bees into the hive. This is a difficult job that you should never try to do yourself. The local beekeeping association might agree to start your colony off with a queen and small swarm.

The hive will have a removable roof or tray, depending on where the honey chambers are located. When it is time to remove the honey, the beekeeper must be completely covered from head to toe in clothing that will protect him or her from bee stings. Special thick gloves and a strong gauze mask or headgear to cover the face are essential. As you can see, beekeepers often look like something from outer space!

Many beekeepers use smoke to calm the bees when it is time to take the honey. Smoke makes bees think they are under attack, so they quickly swallow as much honey as they can to save it. This makes them sleepy and less likely to get angry.

It takes the bees only a few minutes to recover from the effect of the smoke afterward.

As winter approaches, food becomes scarce in the hive. But a caring beekeeper can help by feeding the bees syrup made from ordinary sugar and water as a substitute for nectar.

Helping flowers

The bee is a flower's best friend. This may seem odd, since the bee drinks the flower's nectar and takes away most of its pollen. But it's all part of a clever plan, and the survival of flowers depends on it!

Like other living things, plants reproduce. For this to happen, pollen has to mix with tiny eggs to make seeds. This process is known as *pollination*.

But the flower can't do this by itself — it has no moving parts! So what better form of transportation for the pollen than a furry bee looking for a sweet drink!

As a bee climbs into a flower to gather the nectar with its proboscis, the long hairs on its coat brush up against pollen. It's usually a tight squeeze inside a flower so, on the way out, a lot of the pollen brushes off the bee.

The pollen then falls on those parts of the flower that need to be pollinated to form seeds.

The bee is a lifesaver for trees, too. Pollen from male apple trees, for instance, has to find its way to the female trees. In spring, these trees produce sweet-smelling blossoms that attract bees, so they flit from tree to tree, seeking out the delicious nectar.

grow

Pollen from one tree sticks to the bee's furry body, and some falls off when the bee lands on the next tree. Without the flower's best friend, there would be no fruit trees, either!

19

Swarming

Imagine you're a queen honeybee that's getting a little bit old. You've been so good at laying eggs that there's hardly room to move inside your hive. It's time to go.

But you can't leave before a new queen is raised. She has to be hatched in a special, large cell since, like you, the future queen is going to grow a lot bigger than all the other bees.

When you are ready to leave, you will take some worker bees with you. After all, you can't forage for your own food. The drones, however, will stay behind to mate with the new queen.

All the travelers will leave the hive together, and your swarm will make a dazzling sight. Hundreds of you squeeze tightly together in a buzzing mass of bodies as you fly to a nearby tree and rest.

But where will you go? Before you left the hive, a few scout bees went house-hunting. Once they found what seemed a safe place for a new home, they told all the bees in the swarm where this was by performing a special dance.

Whether it is in a hollow tree, or a nest left by a bird or mouse, you will soon be settled, and your workers will build new combs in which you can lay more eggs. Now all of you have a new home!

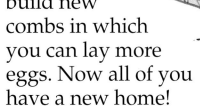

21

Did you know?

▲ *Do all bees live in nests?*
No, a few prefer to live alone, like the brightly colored southern European bee, *above.*

When did the first bees live?
Scientists think some types of bees have been on Earth for about 200 million years.

How far do bees have to travel in order to collect nectar for honey?
Amazingly, for every 2.2 pounds (1 kilogram) of honey that reaches your table, the bees that collected all the nectar flew the equivalent of six times around Earth.

What is royal jelly?
Worker honeybees make royal jelly from glands in their head. They feed it to the larvae for just their first three days of life. But a future queen will eat royal jelly until adulthood.

▼ *What size is the smallest bee that we know – and the biggest?*
The smallest bee lives in the deserts of the southwestern United States, and is about half the size of your little fingernail. The largest is about thirteen times that size, and lives on islands in the southern Pacific Ocean.

How do bees communicate?

Bees create a hum from body movements to pass on information. They also communicate by touching one another's antennae, by dancing, and by producing certain smells.

How long does it take for bees to become adults?

It takes about three weeks for workers and drones to develop. Queens emerge after sixteen days.

Do all bees sting?

Only worker and queen bees sting. Although the bee sting is poisonous, it is usually harmless to humans. However, some people are allergic to bee stings and may become dangerously ill. These individuals require special medicine within a short time of being stung.

Do bees always die after stinging?

When a honeybee stings, it leaves the stinger and part of its body in its victim. It then dies within twenty-four hours. But bumblebees can pull out their stingers and attack again.

How long does a bee live?

Worker bees and drones live from four to six weeks. The queen, however, has a much longer life.

How do bees buzz?

Buzzing is the sound of bees' wings vibrating at great speed as they fly.

▼ Do any other animals eat bees?

Several animals eat bees. Toads wait outside a nest to ambush bees. Bears and the African honey badger, or ratel, *below*, will even break open a nest for dinner.

Glossary

antennae — movable sensory organs on the head of an insect used to touch and smell.

glands — organs that make and release substances such as sweat and saliva.

grub — the larval form of bees and some other insects.

hive — the home of a bee colony, built and looked after by a beekeeper.

larva — the wingless stage of an insect's life between the egg and the pupa.

lens — part of the eye that focuses light rays.

nectar — a sweet liquid produced by flowers and gathered by bees.

pollen — tiny grains that fertilize female plant cells to produce seeds.

proboscis — the long, tubelike mouthpart of a bee used to suck nectar.

pupa — the stage of an insect's life between larva and adult.

Books and Videos

Bees, Wasps, and Ants. George S. Fichler (Western Publishing)

The Fascinating World of Bees. J. M. Parramon (Barron)

Honeybees. James P. Rowan (Rourke)

Killer Bees. Laurence Pringle (Morrow)

The World of Honeybees. Virginia Harrison (Gareth Stevens)

The Bee. (Barr Films video)

Bees: How They Live and Work. (JEF Films video)

Index